D0245578

ACC. No: 02678464

This is my truck

Written by Chris Oxlade
Photography by Andy Crawford

FRANKLIN WATTS
LONDON · SYDNEY

This edition 2009

First published in 2006 by
Franklin Watts
338 Euston Road, London NW1 3BH

Franklin Watts Australia
Hachette Children's Books
Level 17/207 Kent Street, Sydney NSW 2000

Copyright © Franklin Watts 2006

Editor: Jennifer Schofield
Designer: Jemima Lumley
Photography: Andy Crawford
Truck driver: Dave Jackson

Acknowledgements:
All photography by Andy Crawford except p15; p21 top;
p25 courtesy of Eddie Stobart

The Publisher would like to thank Daphne Tweddle, Neale Burdon,
Dave Jackson, Scott Goode and all at Eddie Stobart for their help
in producing this book.

Every attempt has been made to clear copyright. Should there be any inadvertent
omission please apply to the Publisher for rectification.

A CIP catalogue record for this book is available from the British Library.

ISBN: 978 0 7496 8916 2
Dewey Classification: 629'225

Printed in China

Franklin Watts is a division of Hachette Children's Books,
an Hachette Livre UK company.
www.hachettelivre.co.uk

> Contents

> My truck and me

Hello! This mega machine
is a truck. I am a truck driver.

My truck carries things
from place to place.

trailer

tractor

The front part is called a tractor.
The back part is called a trailer.

> The wheels

My truck is very heavy.
It has lots of large wheels.

> *The tyres have grooves to grip the road when it rains.*

∨ *This is the drive shaft. It makes the wheels turn around.*

drive shaft

> Truck power

The truck is moved along by its engine.

< *The engine is under this bonnet. It is big and powerful.*

> *Fuel for the engine is stored in this tank.*

< *Before a long trip, I need to fill up with fuel.*

> Hooking up

The truck's tractor pulls the trailer along.

∧ *I reverse the tractor onto the trailer to hook them together.*

hook

∧ This is the hook on the tractor for a trailer. It is called the fifth wheel.

> These cables and air hoses hook to the trailer. They make the lights and brakes work.

> Trailers

There are lots of different trailers for my tractor to pull.

∧ *This is a curtainside trailer.*
Its sides fold back like a curtain.

V *This is a walking floor trailer. It has a moving floor, so it can unload itself.*

< *This is a motorbike trailer. It is used to take motorbikes to and from races.*

> In the cab

I sit in the cab to drive my truck.

∧ *The cab is full of controls that I use for driving.*

mirror

mirror

< *I look in these big mirrors to see behind the truck.*

> Loading up

Today, I am delivering a curtainside trailer full of packages.

∧ *I hook up the trailer by reversing up to it.*

∨ *The fifth wheel clicks into place.*

< *Next, I connect up the cables and air hoses to the trailer. Now, I am ready to go!*

19

> On the road

I drive along, following
my map.

⋀ *I have a good view of
the road from my cab.*

< If I get tired, I can stop and sleep on the bed in the cab.

I am at the end of my trip. Sometimes, I unhook the trailer and pick up another one.

> **Unloading a trailer**

Now it is time to get out of my cab and unload the packages.

∧ *First, I lower the trailer leg.*

> *Then, I unclip the curtains.*

> *Next, I fold back the curtains.*

∨ *The packages are taken off the truck by a fork lift.*

> More trucks

Here are some more trucks that I drive.

∧ This is a fork lift. It is used for loading and unloading the trailers.

> *This truck is pulling a trailer. It is called a "draw bar" truck.*

∨ *This truck takes rally cars to and from races.*

▷ Be a truck driver

It takes a lot of practice to become a truck driver.

∨ *You have to learn how to drive the heavy truck safely.*

∧ *You need to know how all the parts of the engine work.*

< *You need to learn how the cab controls work, too.*

> Truck parts

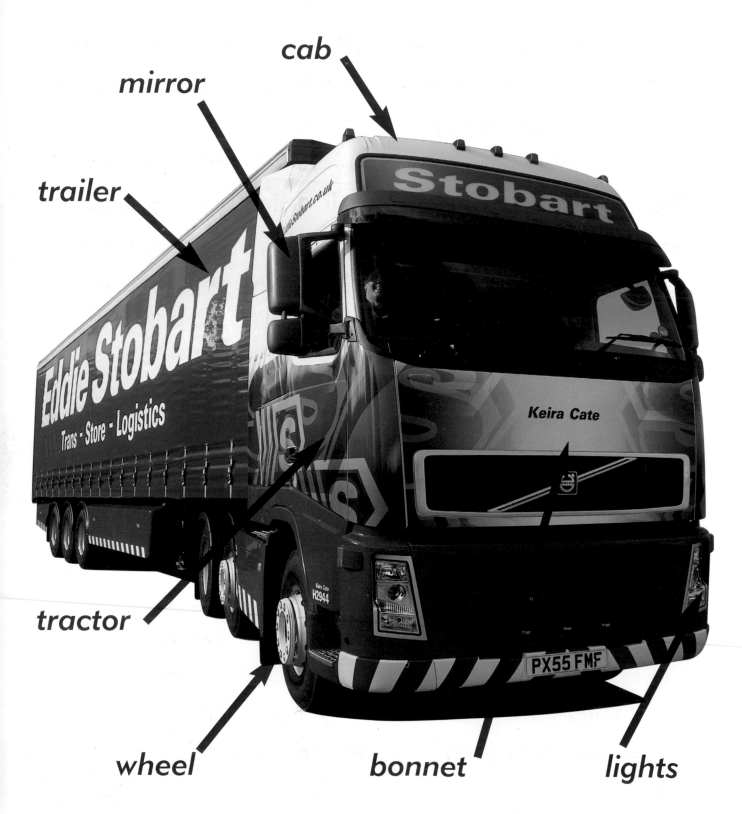

cab

mirror

trailer

tractor

wheel

bonnet

lights

> Word bank

bonnet – the engine's cover

brakes – the part of the truck that slows it down or stops it

connect – to plug in

delivering – taking things from one place to another

engine – the part of a truck that makes it move

fifth wheel – the part of the tractor that hooks up to the trailer

reversing – driving backwards

unloading – taking goods and packages off the trailer

view – what you can see

Websites

Each Eddie Stobart truck has its own girl's name. The truck in this book is called Keira Cate. To find out more about Eddie Stobart trucks or to join the Eddie Stobart Members Club, log on to www.eddiestobart.co.uk

> Index